Deliverance
of the
Firstborn
and
First Sons

Study Guide and Prayer Points

REV. JAMES SOLOMON

ISBN 979-8-88832-748-7 (paperback)
ISBN 979-8-88832-749-4 (digital)

Christian Faith Publishing
832 Park Avenue
Meadville, PA 16335
www.christianfaithpublishing.com

Printed in the United States of America

ACKNOWLEDGEMENT

Discovering the importance of people in the pursuit of greatness is one of the best discoveries we can make in life. It is important to note that from the cradle to the grave, we will always need people who will help us succeed and fulfill our divine destiny.

I want to express my appreciation for some people whom God has placed in my life to help me in my journey toward greatness. This book is a joint effort of people who believe in my vision and have contributed immensely to one area or the other to make it a reality.

I want to declare my appreciation for my father in the Lord, the late Rev. Dr. James Boyejo. Your life and ministry have greatly impacted my life for good. I can't forget you, Pastor Enoch Adeboye—general overseer of the Redeemed Christian Church of God Worldwide and my mentor—whose life and ministry have been a perfect example to me at all times. Sir, I love and appreciate the opportunity given to me to be a blessing to the body of Christ in the Redeemed Christian Church of God Worldwide. Thanks a lot for always being there for me.

I cannot forget my special friend, Rev. Dr. Benson Omomukuyo of Christ's Anointed Kingdom Church, Lagos, Nigeria, and all my faithful pastors who are committed to the vision of Jesus People's Revival Ministries and Jesus Family Chapel in Nigeria, in the United Kingdom, and in the United States of America. I also appreciate those who sacrificed their time and effort on this book, namely Ms. Roli E. Buwa and Pastor Christy Ogbeide. You are such a wonderful blessing in our midst here in America.

Finally, I appreciate the members of my family. May the Lord lift up your heads in life in Jesus's name.

CONTENTS

CHAPTER 1

General Overview of the Firstborn and First Sons

Confession for the Firstborn

- I am a firstborn.
- I am the beginning of strength in my household.
- I am the excellency of dignity and power.
- I shall not be a deficit unto the world.
- I shall be as stable as a rock.
- I shall excel, and no one shall defile me.
- I shall not die a grievous death.
- I shall not be an infant of days, and neither shall I be an adult who has not fulfilled his years.
- I shall have the might of Samson but not his carelessness.
- I shall have the wisdom of Solomon but not his whoredom.
- I shall have the holiness of Job but not his calamities.
- I shall possess the gates of my enemies.
- I shall not be subject to pain or poverty.
- The enemy shall not outwit me.
- The Lord shall anoint me with the oil of gladness above my fellows.
- The fire of the enemy shall not burn me.
- My head shall not be buried in shame.

- I shall be respected and honored in my father's house.
- I shall be first among equals and preferred among many.
- As a firstborn, I redeem my destiny by the precious blood of Jesus.
- I dedicate myself this day to the God of Abraham, Isaac, and Jacob, and the Father of our Lord Jesus Christ. Amen.

Facts about the Firstborn

1. Firstborn children are welcome into a tightly primped environment diddled with elevated standards and high expectations.
2. Firstborn children are negatively affected, and they are children with adult problems; alone and young, they must overcome their sentence being an older brother or sister, but to the younger, they are parents; some left school early to become interim, carrying on all household responsibility and expenses.
3. Amateur parents' inevitable anxiety can often slip into a first-born, resulting in a lifetime of worry and self-consciousness.
4. The firstborn carries the curses of harm from parents and has to erase the stain and transmit blessings to their other siblings and to the next generation.
5. On the optimistic side, firstborn children often develop a diverse vocabulary at an early age; they are independent, strong-willed, and able to adapt easily in many situations.
6. The firstborn is known to be highly organized; he is confi-dent, determined because the family depends on him, and is good in finishing projects or completing tasks.
7. The firstborn often is an excellent leader as he/she gets early training in being the boss when babysitting and taking care of the house.
8. The firstborn is eager to place, as well as pursue careers in education, politics, and entrepreneurship.
9. The firstborn often takes the role of "peacemaker," attempt-ing to resolve financial and all kinds of problems. He/she

mediates and abstains from initiating more conflict, as this can lead to perpetual passive aggressiveness.

10. Firstborn children tend to be overachievers and can be greatly discouraged by perceived failures relating to school, career, or personal relationships.

11. Newscasters or TV talk show hosts tend to be firstborn or only children. Prominent examples include Walter Cronkite, Peter Jennings, Dan Rather, Ted Koppel, Oprah Winfrey, Geraldo Rivera, Arsenio Hall, and Rush Limbaugh.

12. Over half of US presidents are firstborn, including Barrack and Michelle Obama. Firstborn children are overrepresented among Nobel Prize winners.

More facts…

> Reuben, thou art my firstborn, my might,
> and the beginning of my strength, the excellency
> of dignity, and the excellency of power: Unstable
> as water, thou shalt not excel; because thou
> wentest up to thy father's bed, then defiledst thou
> it: he went up to my couch. (Genesis 49:3–4)

Every family needs this deliverance. There is no family without a firstborn male child. Firstborn males are a total disappointment to the family and community. The truth is, Adam, the firstborn of God, was driven out of God's presence, care, provision, protection, and supervision, and so are most firstborn males. They never concentrate on anything that will lead to a bright future and are always roaming from place to place.

After Adam, Cain—the firstborn of Adam—became a murderer. Later Cain left the presence of God and wandered eastward. Thereafter, Noah cursed Canaan, the firstborn of Ham, saying that he will be a servant of servants. Next, the firstborn of Jacob, Reuben, was cursed with being "unstable as water," to put it superficially. As a result, most firstborn males tend to resemble all that had been pronounced on firstborn males—unworthy, worthless lifestyles, unstable, always roaming about, cannot hold down a job or trade, wayward, riotous, and mostly failures in life.

The firstborn male is usually the spiritual inheritor of his father's legacy—good or bad—especially in the African tradition! This means that he inherits the blessings or curses, the holy or evil altars, wars or peace, problems or solutions, riches or poverty, and so on. As a result of these equations, firstborn males require special favor from God to prosper in life. The only way out of this seemingly evil inheritance is to be born again in Christ Jesus!

> The Lord is longsuffering, and of great mercy, forgiving iniquity and transgression, and by no means clearing the guilty, visiting the iniquity of the fathers upon the children unto the third and fourth generation. (Numbers 14:18)

God Himself has said in the Old Testament of the Bible that He would visit the iniquities of the fathers upon their upcoming generations. The only thing that can effectively exempt us from this wrath of God is the BLOOD OF JESUS!

> Thus saith the Lord, Israel is my son, even my firstborn… (Exodus 4: 22)

The above verse shows that in a spiritual sense, God considers the nation of Israel His firstborn among all nations. This is very interesting because the tribe's namesake, Jacob, was NOT the firstborn of his father, Isaac. He was born second because his brother, Esau, muscled him out of the way and emerged first from the womb. Nonetheless, though he was the younger, Israel still received the blessing of the firstborn. This is just one instance of a common biblical principle stated by Jesus as follows:

> But many that are first shall be last; and the last shall be first. (Matthew 19:30)

The very same thing happened to Jacob's firstborn son, Reuben. From his deathbed, Jacob prophesied over Reuben.

> Reuben, thou art my firstborn, my might,
> and the beginning of my strength, the excellency
> of dignity, and the excellency of power:
> Unstable as water, thou shalt not excel;
> because thou wentest up to thy father's bed;
> then defiledst thou it: he went up to my couch.
> (Genesis 49:3–4)

Since spiritually the nation of Israel is God's firstborn, Israel should receive a corresponding spiritual blessing. However, spiritually Israel was NOT blessed, just as Esau and Reuben were not blessed. Both Esau and Reuben defaulted on their rightful inheritance because of their unrighteousness. Just so, the nation of Israel, which was God's spiritual firstborn, defaulted on its rightful spiritual inheritance because for the most part it rejected the only true righteousness, which is found in Christ **(Acts 13:46)**. We should NOT think of Israel as a specially blessed nation any more than Reuben was a specially blessed son of Israel or Esau was a specially blessed son of Esau.

The blessing of God's spiritual firstborn was bestowed on another nation, not upon Israel. Which nation? Here God did something completely new. He created a spiritual nation for Himself, which comprised of people from "every kindred and tongue and people and nation" **(Revelation 5:9)**, which is His "Church of the firstborn" **(Hebrews 12:23)**. The greater part of this holy nation comes from the Gentiles, not from God's "firstborn" nation Israel **(Romans 9:30–31, Galatians 3:14)**. The Gentiles received this blessing initially through the ministry of Paul, a Jew of the tribe of Benjamin (the LAST-BORN son of Israel). Paul described himself as an apostle "born out of due time," yet he labored more fruitfully than all the other apostles **(1 Corinthians 15:8, 10)**. Paul's motivation was to make God's blessing of the Gentiles manifest so that Israel would see and follow the Gentiles' example **(Romans 11:11–14)**. Once again, we see "the last shall be first, and the first shall be last."

We've said repeatedly that there is a systematic biblical principle that the firstborn son does NOT receive the blessing due the firstborn, but instead the last shall be first, and the first shall be last. This principle is demonstrated ultimately in Jesus Christ in two distinct ways. For as Son of Man, He was the last Adam, yet He was blessed above the first Adam **(1 Corinthians 15:45–49)**. But as the only begotten Son of God, He was the firstborn, yet He took a curse upon Himself **(Galatians 3:13)**. He did this not because He deserved it (as Esau and Reuben did) but willingly, that we might also share in the same blessings as God's firstborn.

CHAPTER 2

Biblical Overview of the Firstborn

Challenges Confronting the Firstborn

A firstborn son held a special place in ancient families (**Genesis 49:3**). His was the birthright, which included three great benefits.

I. The leadership of the clan upon his father's demise (**Genesis 27:29, 49:3**)
II. A double portion of the inheritance (**Genesis 48:22, Deuteronomy 21:17**)
III. The status of the family's priest—the spiritual head by whom the covenant relationship with God was perpetuated (**Genesis 8:20, 12:8**)

With Abraham, Isaac, and Jacob, God established a spiritual dynasty upon which was based the later expectations of Israel (**Exodus 3:6**), but these privileges could be withdrawn.

Reuben forfeited his birthright by an immoral act (**Genesis 49:4, 1 Chronicles 5:1**); Esau forfeited his birthright by a profane attitude (**Genesis 25:32–34, Hebrews 12:16**).

In the process of time, the emphasis of birthright privileges was shifted from primogeniture to moral excellence. It is remarkable how many "firstborn" in the Bible had to take a lesser place because better men were exalted to prominence by God. Abel was preferred to Cain

(Genesis 4:3–7, Hebrews 11:4); Japheth was the eldest son of Noah **(Genesis 10:21)**; yet in all the lists, Shem (father of the Semitic races) comes first **(Genesis 5:32, 10:1)**. Abraham was the younger son of Terah, yet as Dr. Robert Jamieson says, *"Although in the enumeration of his sons, Abram, like Shem, is from his great eminence mentioned first, he was not the eldest of the family. That honor belonged not to him, but to Haran* **(Genesis 11:29)**.*"* Jacob was preferred to Esau **(Malachi 1:2)** and obtained God's approval.

Reuben ("unstable as water") lost his birthright. The benefits were distributed among the other sons of Jacob. Judah ("the scepter") received tribal leadership **(Genesis 49:10)**, and Joseph was blessed with double portion **(Genesis 49:26)**. Levi, though "scattered in Israel" (that is without tribal lands), eventually obtained priestly status by the sovereign decision of God **(Exodus 28:1)**, which was confirmed by their faithful stand against idolatry at Horeb **(Exodus 32:26–29)**. His curse became a blessing, as his name implies (Levi means "to join together"). The tribe became a uniting influence throughout the whole of Israel in its ritual and teaching ministry **(2 Chronicles 35:3)**. They served to keep Israel spiritually alive.

Perhaps the most outstanding case is David. He was the youngest of eight sons **(1 Samuel 16:10–13)**. Samuel was directed in a vision to the household of Jesse the Bethlehemite and dramatically instructed to anoint David for kingship. Red-haired, handsome, athletic, yet despised by his older brothers **(1 Samuel 17:28)**, he, nevertheless, was adopted by God as His firstborn **(Psalm 89:27)**.

The emphasis upon character fitness rather than chronological fact is very significant. In such cases, the birthright has nothing to do with time but with worth. And in this light, we may explain the use of the term *firstborn* with regard to our Lord Jesus Christ. He is the "firstborn of every creature" **(Colossians 1:15)**—that is, not only is He the Creator and Heir of all things **(Hebrews 1:2)**, but He is also Lord of all things **(Matthew 28:18)**. He is also the "firstborn from the dead" **(Colossians 1:18)**; not the first to rise but the greatest to rise; not only Conqueror over the tomb but also able to deliver us from death, and even from dying **(John 11:25–26, 14:19; 1 Corinthians 15:20, 45)**. He is the "firstborn among many brethren" **(Romans 8:29)**;

"Head of the Body—the Church" **(Ephesians 1:22, Colossians 1:18)**, who with Him are "heirs of God and joint-heirs with Christ" **(Romans 8:17)**, sharing His throne **(Revelation 3:21)**, and as the "Church of the firstborn, which are written in Heaven…" **(Hebrews 12:23)**, reigning in life forever "by one, Jesus Christ" **(Romans 5:17)**. The Church of Jesus Christ is not the first of God's chosen people; that honor belongs to Israel—"to the Jews first" (Romans 1:16)—but though the Church may not be the first, it certainly is the foremost in God's plans. We are exalted in Christ above all height, "set among princes and made to inherit the throne of glory…" (1 Samuel 2:8)

> Who is like unto the Lord our God, Who dwelleth on high, Who humbleth Himself to behold the things that are in Heaven, and in the earth! He raiseth up the poor out of the dust, and lifteth the needy out of the dunghill; That He may set him with princes, even with the princes of his people. (Psalm 113:5–8)

> And the Lord shall make thee the head and not the tail; and thou shalt be above only, and thou shalt not be beneath; if that thou hearken unto the commandments of the Lord thy God, which I command thee this day, to observe and to do them. (Deuteronomy 28:13)

> Yea, the Almighty shall be thy defence, and thou shalt have plenty of silver. For then shalt thou have thy delight in the Almighty, and shalt lift up thy face unto God. Thou shalt pay thy vows. Thou shalt also decree a thing, and it shall be established unto thee: and the light shall shine upon thy ways. (Job 22:25–28)

> And now shall mine head be lifted up above mine enemies round about me: therefore will I

offer in His tabernacle sacrifices of joy; I will sing,
yea, I will sing praise unto the Lord. (Psalm 27:6)

The Old Testament

The Hebrew word found in many Semitic languages has the general meaning "to be early"; firstborn is used for people and animals. Cognate terms are also being employed for firstfruits and the firstborn son's privileges and responsibilities—also known as his "birthright." In **Genesis 25:23**, the eldest son is called *rab£*, a description occurring elsewhere only in the second millennium cuneiform texts.

The firstborn was regarded as "the beginning of his strength" **(Genesis 49:3; Deuteronomy 21:17; Psalm78:51, 105:36)** and "the opener of the womb" **(Exodus 13:2, 12, 15; Numbers 18:15)**, emphasizing both paternal and maternal lines. The preeminent status of firstborn was also accorded to Israel **(Exodus 4:22)** and the Davidic line **(Psalm 89:27)**.

The eldest son's special position was widely recognized in the ancient Near East, though it was not usually extended to sons of concubines or female slaves **(Genesis 21:9–13, Judges 11:1–2)**. The accompanying privileges were highly valued, and included in the Old Testament was a larger inheritance, a special paternal blessing, family leadership, and an honored place at mealtimes **(Genesis 25:5–6, 27:35–36, 37:21, 42:37, 43:33; Deuteronomy 21:15–17)**. The double inheritance of **Deuteronomy 21:15–17**, though apparently unknown to the Patriarchs **(Genesis 25:5–6)**, is mentioned in several old Babylonian, Middle Assyrian, and Nuzi documents and is alluded to elsewhere in the Old Testament **(2 Kings 2:9, Isaiah 61:7)**.

These privileges could normally be forfeited only by committing a serious offense **(Genesis 35:22, 49:4; 1 Chronicles 5:1–2)** or by sale **(Genesis 25:29–34)**, though paternal preference occasionally overruled in the matter of royal succession **(1 Kings 1 and 2, 2 Chronicles 11:22–23, 1 Chronicles 26:10)**. There is also a marked interest, especially in the book of Genesis, in the youngest son (e.g., Jacob, Ephraim, Isaac, Joseph, David), but such cases were certainly contrary to expectation **(Genesis 48:17, 1 Samuel 16:6)**.

Where there were no sons, the eldest daughter took responsibility for her younger sisters **(Genesis 19:30)**. It was an Aramaean custom **(Genesis 29:26)** and perhaps an Israelite one too **(1 Samuel 18:17–27)** for the eldest daughter to be married first. An Ugaritic text mentions the transfer of birthright from the eldest to the youngest daughter.

In an Israelite custom, the firstborn of a man and a beast has a special place. The firstborn male belonged to Yahweh **(Exodus 13:2, 22:29–20; Numbers 3:13)**, and this was underlined by Israel's deliverance in the final plague. Children were redeemed in the Exodus generation by the Levites **(Numbers 3:40–41)** and later at one month old by a payment of five shekels **(Numbers 18:16, 3:42–51)**. Human sacrifice of the firstborn is occasionally mentioned, following Canaanite practice **(2 Kings 3:27; Ezekiel 20:25–26; Micah 6:7; 1 Kings 16:34)**, but this was a misinterpretation of **Exodus 22:29**. Clean male firstlings were sacrificed **(Numbers 18:17–18; Deuteronomy 12:6, 17)**, while imperfect animals were eaten in the towns **(Deuteronomy 15:21–23)**. Male firstlings of unclean animals were redeemed **(Numbers 18:15)**, though an ass was redeemed with a lamb or had its neck broken **(Exodus 13:13, 34:20)**.

The New Testament

Jesus was the firstborn of His mother **(Matthew 1:25, Luke 2:7)**, a phrase which allows but does not demand that Mary had other children **(Mark 6:3)**. As such, Jesus was taken to the temple by Mary and Joseph to be offered to God **(Luke 2:22–24)**. Since Luke omits mentioning of any price being paid to redeem the Child, he may have intended the incident to be regarded as the dedication of the firstborn to the service of God **(1 Samuel 1:11, 22, 28)**. Jesus is also the firstborn of His heavenly Father. He is the firstborn of all creation, not in the sense that He Himself is a created being but rather that as God's Son, He was His agent in creation and hence has authority over all created things **(Colossians 1:15–17)**.

Similarly, He is the firstborn in the new creation by being the first to be raised from the dead and is thus Lord over the Church

(Colossians 1:18, Revelation 1:5). He is the firstborn in a whole family of God's children who are destined to bear His image **(Romans 8:29)**. There may be an echo of **Psalm 89:27** in **Hebrews 1:6**, where God's Son is the object of worship by the angels at His coming into the world (whether the incarnation, resurrection, or second coming). Finally, God's people, both living and dead, can be described as the firstborn who are enrolled in heaven, since they partake in the privileges of the Son (Hebrews 12:23).

CHAPTER 3

Discovering the Firstborn

What is the significance of the "firstborn" in the Bible? In the Old Testament, the firstborn son was the one who normally received a double inheritance and was the one who would inherit his father's role as head of the family, although God sometimes reversed this order, like he did with Jacob and Esau **(Genesis 25:21–26)** and as Jacob later did with Ephraim and Manasseh **(Genesis 48:13–22)**. Reuben was the firstborn of Jacob, but his rights as the firstborn were taken away because of his sin **(Genesis 35:22, 49:3–4)**.

The term *firstborn*, therefore, has two main meanings. The first is more literal, referring to the fact that this son is the first son born to his father. The second meaning refers to the rights and authority of a person because they are the firstborn. Our Lord Jesus is the "firstborn" in several ways, but most of all, He is the One Who has been appointed by God to be in authority over ALL things **(Colossians 1:13–23)**.

Closely related is the word *son* as seen in the following verses:

> I will be his father, and he shall be my <u>son</u>.
> If he commits iniquity, I will chasten him with
> the rod of men, and with the stripes of the chil-
> dren of men. (2 Samuel 7:14)

> I will declare the decree: the LORD hath
> said unto me, Thou art my Son; this day have I

begotten thee. Ask of me, and I shall give thee the heathen for thine inheritance, and the uttermost parts of the earth for thy possession. Thou shalt break them with a rod of iron; thou shalt dash them in pieces like a potter's vessel. (Psalm 2:7–9)

As compared with **Psalm 110:1–3 and Hebrews 1:5–14**, the expressions in the following verses are synonymous:

Thou art my Son, this day have I begotten thee… (Hebrews 1:5a)

I will be to him a Father, and he shall be to me a Son… (Hebrews 1:5b)

This speaks not of the birth of our Lord (as though this was when He came into existence—for He is eternal as **John 1:1–3** indicates) but of His installation as King of the earth by His Father.

First Begotten

The Greek word *Prototokos* is translated in two passages in the King James Version as "first begotten."

And again, when he bringeth in the first-begotten into the world, he saith, And let all the angels of God worship him. (Hebrews 1:6)

And from Jesus Christ, who is the faithful witness, and the first begotten of the dead, and the prince of the kings of the earth. Unto him that loved us, and washed us from our sins in his own blood… (Revelation 1:5)

However, in all other places in the King James Version and in the Revised Version (British and American), it is translated as "firstborn." This word was used to describe Jesus Christ in the literal sense as Mary's firstborn.

> And she brought forth her firstborn son, and wrapped him in swaddling clothes, and laid him in a manger; because there was no room for them in the inn. (Luke 2:7)

> And knew her not till she had brought forth her firstborn son: and he called his name JESUS. (Matthew 1:25)

It also bears the literal sense of the firstborn of men and animals, as in:

> Through faith he kept the passover, and the sprinkling of blood, lest he that destroyed the firstborn should touch them. (Hebrews 11:28)

Metaphorically, it is used of Jesus Christ to express His relation to man and the universe and His difference from them, as both He and they are related to God. The laws and customs of all nations show that to be "firstborn" means not only priority in time but a certain superiority in privilege and authority. Israel is Yahweh's firstborn among the nations.

> And thou shalt say unto Pharaoh, Thus saith the LORD, Israel is my son, even my firstborn. (Exodus 4:22)

> They shall come with weeping, and with supplications will I lead them: I will cause them to walk by the rivers of waters in a straight way, wherein they shall not stumble: for I am a father to Israel, and Ephraim is my firstborn. (Jeremiah 31:9)

The Messianic King is God's firstborn.

> Also I will make him my firstborn, higher
> than the kings of the earth. (Psalm 89:27).

Christ as "the firstborn of all creation" **(Colossians 1:15)** is not only prior in time but above in power and authority.

> All things were created by him, and for
> him… (Colossians 1:16)

He is "sovereign Lord over all creation by virtue of primo-geniture" (Lightfoot). It denotes His status and character and not His origin; the context does not admit the idea that He is a part of the created universe. So in His incarnation, He is brought into the world as "firstborn," and God summons all His angels to worship Him **(Hebrews 1:6)**. In His resurrection, He is "firstborn from the dead" **(Colossians 1:18)** or "of the dead" **(Revelation 1:5)**, the origin and prince of life. And finally, He is the "firstborn among many brethren" in the consummation of God's purpose of grace when all the elect are gathered home. He is not only their Lord but also their pattern, God's ideal Son, and men are foreordained to be conformed to His image" **(Romans 8:29)**. Therefore, the saints themselves, as growing in His likeness and as possessing all the privileges of eldest sons, including the kingdom and priesthood, may be called the "church of the firstborn who are enrolled in heaven" **(Hebrews 12:23)**.

Firstborn! Firstling!

The Hebrew word for firstborn and firstling (*bekhor, prototokos*) denotes the firstborn of human beings as well as of animals.

> And all the firstborn in the land of Egypt
> shall die, from the first born of Pharaoh that sit-
> teth upon his throne, even unto the firstborn of

the maidservant that is behind the mill; and all
the firstborn of beasts. (Exodus 11:5)

Meanwhile, a word from the same root denotes firstfruits.

> And the feast of harvest, the firstfruits of thy
> labours, which thou hast sown in the field: and
> the feast of ingathering, which is in the end of the
> year, when thou hast gathered in thy labours out
> of the field. (Exodus 23:16)

All the data point to the conclusion that among the ancestors of
the Hebrews, the sacrifice of the firstborn was practiced, just as the
firstlings of the flocks and the firstfruits of the produce of the earth
were devoted to the deity. The narrative of the Moabite war records
the sacrifice of the heir to the throne by Mesha to Chemosh, the
national god.

> Then he took his eldest son that should
> have reigned in his stead and offered him for a
> burnt offering upon the wall. And there was great
> indignation against Israel: and they departed
> from hi and returned to their own land. (2 Kings
> 3:27)

This barbaric custom must have become extinct at an early
period in the religion of Israel.

> And he said, Lay not thine hand upon the
> lad, neither do thou anything unto him: for now
> I know that thou fearest God, seeing thou hast
> not withheld thy son, thine only son from me.
> (Genesis 22:12)

It was probably due to the influence of surrounding nations
that the cruel practice was revived toward the close of the monar-

chical *period* (**2 Kings 16:3, 17:17, 2 Kings 21:6; Jeremiah 7:31; Ezekiel 16:20, 23:37; Micah 6:7**).

Jeremiah denies that the offering of human beings could have been an instruction from Yahweh (**Jeremiah 7:31, 19:5**). The prophetic conception that God had rendered such a doctrine is inconceivable. Clear evidence of the spiritualization and humanization of religion among the Israelites is furnished in the replacement at an early stage of the actual sacrifice of the firstborn by their dedication to the service of Yahweh. At a later stage, the Levites were substituted for the firstborn. Just as the firstlings of unclean animals were redeemed with money (**Exodus 13:13, Exodus 34:20**), the dedication of the firstborn was substituted with the consecration of the Levites to the service of the sanctuary (**Numbers 3:11–13, 15**). On the thirtieth day after birth, the firstborn was brought to the priest by his father who paid five shekels for the child's redemption from service in the temple. For that service, the Levites were accepted in place of the redeemed firstborn (**Numbers 3:45**).

According **to Exodus 22:29–31**, the firstborn is given to Yahweh. The firstborn of clean animals, if free from spot or blemish, was to be sacrificed after eight days (**Numbers 18:17**). This allusion to the sacrifice of the firstborn as part of the religion of Yahweh has been variously explained. Some scholars suspect the text, but in all probability, the verse means no more than similar references to the fact that the firstborn belonged to Yahweh (**Exodus 13:2, 34:19**). The modifying clause with regard to the redemption of the firstborn has been omitted.

The firstborn possessed the definite privileges which were denied other members of the family. The law forbade the disinheriting of the firstborn (**Deuteronomy 21:15–17**). Such legislation in polygamous times was necessary to prevent a favorite wife from exercising undue influence over her husband in distributing his property as in the case of Jacob (**Genesis 25:23**). The oldest son's share was twice as large as that of any other son. When Elisha prayed for a double portion of Elijah's spirit, he simply wished to be considered the firstborn (i.e., the successor of the dying prophet).

Yahweh's firstborn **(Exodus 4:22)**, Israel, as compared to other nations, was entitled to special privileges. She occupied a unique position in virtue of the special relationship between Yahweh and the nation. In three passages, Jesus Christ is the firstborn among many brethren **(Romans 8:29)**, of every creature **(Colossians 1:16)**, brought into the world **(Hebrews 1:6)**. This application of terms to Jesus Christ can be traced back **to Psalms 89:27**, where the Davidic ruler or perhaps the nation is alluded to as the firstborn of Yahweh.

CHAPTER 4

Errors of the Firstborn—Scriptural References

And Lot went up out of Zoar, and dwelt in the mountain, and his two daughters with him; for he feared to dwell in Zoar: and he dwelt in a cave, he and his two daughters.

And the firstborn said unto the younger, "Our father is old, and there is not a man in the earth to come in unto us after the manner of all the earth: Come, let us make our father drink wine, and we will lie with him, that we may preserve seed of our father."

And they made their father drink wine that night: and the firstborn went in, and lay with her father; and he perceived not when she lay down, nor when she arose.

And it came to pass on the morrow, that the firstborn said unto the younger, Behold, I lay yesternight with my father: let us make him drink wine this night also; and go thou in, and lie with him, that we may preserve seed of our father.

And they made their father drink wine that night also: and the younger arose, and lay with him; and he perceived not when she lay down, nor when she arose.

Thus were both the daughters of Lot with child by their father.

And the first born bare a son and called his name Moab: the same is the father of the Moabites unto this day.

And the younger, she also bare a son, and called his name Benammi: the same is the father of the children of Ammon unto this day. (Genesis 19:3–38)

Birthright of the Firstborn

And they sat before him, the firstborn according to his birthright, and the youngest according to his youth: and the men marvelled one at another.

And he took and sent messes unto them from before him: but Benjamin's mess was five times so much as any of theirs. And they drank and were merry with him. (Genesis 43:33–34)

And Israel stretched out his right hand, and laid it upon Ephraim's head, who was the younger, and his left hand upon Manasseh's head, guiding his hands wittingly; for Manasseh was the firstborn.

And he blessed Joseph, and said, God, before whom my fathers Abraham and Isaac did walk, the God which fed me all my life long unto this day. (Genesis 48:14–15)

For I will pass through the land of Egypt this night, and will smite all the firstborn in the land of Egypt, both man and beast; and against all the gods of Egypt I will execute judgment: I am the LORD. (Exodus 12:12)

And when Joseph saw that his father laid his right hand upon the head of Ephraim, it displeased him: and he held up his father's hand, to remove it from Ephraim's head unto Manasseh's head.

And Joseph said unto his father, "Not so, my father: for this is the firstborn; put thy right hand upon his head."

And his father refused and said, "I know it, my son, I know it: he also shall become a people, and he also shall be great: but truly his younger brother shall be greater than he, and his seed shall become a multitude of nations." (Genesis 48:17–19)

Reuben, thou art my firstborn, my might, and the beginning of my strength, the excellency of dignity, and the excellency of power:

Unstable as water, thou shalt not excel; because thou wentest up to thy father's bed; then defiledst thou it: he went up to my couch. (Genesis 49:3–4)

God's Pronouncement on the Firstborn

And the children struggled together within her; and she said, "If it be so, why am I thus?" And she went to enquire of the LORD.

And the LORD said unto her, "Two nations are in thy womb, and two manner of people shall be separated from thy bowels; and the one people shall be stronger than the other people; and the elder shall serve the younger." (Genesis 25:22–23 KJV)

And the LORD told her, "The sons in your womb will become two nations. From the very beginning, the two nations will be rivals. One nation will be stronger than the other; and your older son will serve your younger son" (Genesis 25:23 NLT)

And Er, Judah's firstborn, was wicked in the sight of the LORD; and the LORD slew him. (Genesis 38:7)

And Joseph called the name of the firstborn Manasseh: For God, said he, hath made me forget all my toil, and all my father's house. (Genesis 41:51)

And it came to pass, that at midnight the LORD smote all the firstborn in the land of Egypt, from the firstborn of Pharaoh that sat on his throne unto the firstborn of the captive that was in the dungeon; and all the firstborn of cattle. (Exodus 12:29)

And Joshua adjured them at that time, saying, Cursed be the man before the LORD, that riseth up and buildeth this city Jericho: he shall lay the foundation thereof in his firstborn, and in his youngest son shall he set up the gates of it. (Joshua 6:26)

And unto David were sons born in Hebron: and his firstborn was Amnon, of Ahinoam the Jezreelitess. (2 Samuel 3:2)

The sons of Judah; Er, and Onan, and Shelah: which three were born unto him of the daughter of Shua the Canaanitess. And Er, the

firstborn of Judah, was evil in the sight of the
LORD; and he slew him. (1 Chronicles 2:3)

The Custom of Redemption

The custom of redeeming the firstborn son is preserved among
the Jews to this day. After thirty days, the father invites the *kohen*
(i.e., a supposedly descendant of Aaron) to the house. The child is
brought and shown to the kohen, and the father declares the mother
of the child to be an Israelite. If she is a kohen, redemption is not
necessary. The kohen asks the father which option he prefers—his
child or the five shekels. The father responds that he prefers his son
and pays the kohen the equivalent of five shekels. After receiving the
redemption money, the kohen puts his hands on the child's head and
pronounces the "Aaronite blessing" **(Numbers 6:22–27)**.

We, therefore, conclude that in **Colossians 1:15**, the phrase
"proftotokos pasefs ktiseofs" is predicated to the preexistent Christ.
Its thrust is to ascribe to Him the primacy of status over all of creation. This status is summarized by saying that He is God's heir par
excellence. The heirship is predicated upon His role in creation, pres-
ervation, and teleology. Behind the predication lies Paul's theological
conception of Christ as the second Adam. While sovereignty is the
keynote of the expression and is placed in juxtaposition with creation,
one must recall the Old Testament and intertestamental usages that
demonstrate overtones of special privilege and affection when the
term is used as a title. That this latter nuance is completely lacking
in **Colossians 1:15** does not follow at all. Indeed, an Old Testament
illustration suffices to guard against such a conclusion.

In **Genesis 22:2**, Isaac is styled as the "beloved son," and the
ensuing narrative also informs us that it was to him that Abraham
gave all he had since Isaac was his heir **(Genesis 24:36, 25:5)**. The
point is simply this: it is artificial to say that *"eikofn"* refers only
to Christ's relationship to the Father and *"proftotokos"* refers only
to creation. Since both terms depict Jesus Christ as the second
Adam, He is thereby brought into relationship with both God the
Father and creation. What does not seem to be present in Paul's use

of "*proftotokos*" is any notion of an "eternal generation" from the Father. This is reading back into the text of the dogmatic reflections of later theologians—reflections that are legitimate but not intended by the apostle Paul's diction.

The predication of Christ as the firstborn in the New Testament offers a challenge to Christologies, ancient and modern. One cannot help being impressed by the scope of this title. At His incarnation **(Luke 2:7)**, Jesus is designated as Mary's firstborn, an appellative connoting His consecration to God and possibly His rightful claim to the Davidic throne. By His glorious resurrection in which He was victorious over sin and death, He became the "firstborn from the dead" **(Colossians 1:18)** and now exercises sovereign sway over His redeemed people as the "firstborn of the dead" **(Revelation 1:5)**.

As the head of a new redeemed humanity destined in the eschatological transfiguration to bear the impress of His image, He is the "firstborn among many brothers" **(Romans 8:29)**. But the conception moves not only forward toward consummation but also, in the thought of Paul, backward into the realm of proctology **(Colossians 1:17)**. In Paul's view, all creation finds its reference point with respect to the "firstborn over all creation," "the heir of all things" **(Colossians 1:15; Hebrews 1:2, 6)**. Indeed, in the eschaton, Christ is the integration point of all things **(Ephesians 1:10)**. A Christology that falls short of this all-encompassing affirmation does not do justice to the scriptural data.

CHAPTER 5

Redemption of the Firstborn

The Firstborn Must Be Redeemed
or Dedicated to God

Thou shalt not delay to offer the first of thy ripe fruits, and of thy liquors: the firstborn of thy sons shalt thou give unto me. (Exodus 22:29)

But the firstling of an ass thou shalt redeem with a lamb: and if thou redeem him not, then shalt thou break his neck. All the firstborn of thy sons thou shalt redeem. And none shall appear before me empty. (Exodus 34:20)

And I, behold, I have taken the Levites from among the children of Israel instead of all the firstborn that openeth the matrix among the children of Israel: therefore the Levites shall be mine;

Because all the firstborn are mine; for on the day that I smote all the firstborn in the land of Egypt I hallowed unto me all the firstborn in Israel, both man and beast: mine shall they be: I am the LORD. (Numbers 3:12–13)

And thou shalt take the Levites for me (I am the LORD) instead of all the firstborn among the children of Israel; and the cattle of the Levites instead of all the firstlings among the cattle of the children of Israel.

And Moses numbered, as the LORD commanded him, all the firstborn among the children of Israel.

And all the firstborn males by the number of names, from a month old and upward, of those that were numbered of them, were twenty and two thousand two hundred and threescore and thirteen.

And the LORD spake unto Moses, saying,

Take the Levites instead of all the firstborn among the children of Israel, and the cattle of the Levites instead of their cattle; and the Levites shall be mine: I am the LORD.

And for those that are to be redeemed of the two hundred and threescore and thirteen of the firstborn of the children of Israel, which are more than the Levites;

Thou shalt even take five shekels apiece by the poll, after the shekel of the sanctuary shalt thou take them: (the shekel is twenty gerahs:)

And thou shalt give the money, wherewith the odd number of them is to be redeemed, unto Aaron and to his sons.

And Moses took the redemption money of them that were over and above them that were redeemed by the Levites:

Of the firstborn of the children of Israel took he the money; a thousand three hundred and threescore and five shekels, after the shekel of the sanctuary:

And Moses gave the money of them that were redeemed unto Aaron and to his sons, according to the word of the Lord, as the Lord commanded Moses. (Numbers 3:41–51)

For they are wholly given unto me from among the children of Israel; instead of such as open every womb, even instead of the firstborn of all the children of Israel, have I taken them unto me.'
For all the firstborn of the children of Israel are mine, both man and beast: on the day that I smote every firstborn in the land of Egypt I sanctified them for myself. (Numbers 8:16–17)

Everything that openeth the matrix in all flesh, which they bring unto the LORD, whether it be of men or beasts, shall be thine: nevertheless the firstborn of man shalt thou surely redeem, and the firstling of unclean beasts shalt thou redeem.
And those that are to be redeemed from a month old shalt thou redeem, according to thine estimation, for the money of five shekels, after the shekel of the sanctuary, which is twenty gerahs. (Numbers 18:15–16)

Now the sons of Reuben the firstborn of Israel, (for he was the firstborn; but forasmuch as he defiled his father's bed, his birthright was given unto the sons of Joseph the son of Israel: and the genealogy is not to be reckoned after the birthright. (1 Chronicles 5:1)

Also the firstborn of our sons, and of our cattle, as it is written in the law, and the firstlings of our herds and of our flocks, to bring to the house of our God, unto the priests that minister in the house of our God:

And that we should bring the firstfruits of our dough, and our offerings, and the fruit of all manner of trees, of wine and of oil, unto the priests, to the chambers of the house of our God; and the tithes of our ground unto the Levites, that the same Levites might have the tithes in all the cities of our tillage.

And the priest the son of Aaron shall be with the Levites, when the Levites take tithes: and the Levites shall bring up the tithe of the tithes unto the house of our God, to the chambers, into the treasure house. (Nehemiah 10:36–38)

Jesus Christ the Firstborn

And knew her not till she had brought forth her firstborn son: and he called his name JESUS. (Matthew 1:25)

For whom he did foreknow, he also did predestinate to be conformed to the image of his Son, that he might be the firstborn among many brethren. (Romans 8:29)

Who is the image of the invisible God, the firstborn of every creature. (Colossians 1:15)

Through faith he kept the passover, and the sprinkling of blood, lest he that destroyed the firstborn should touch them. (Hebrews 11:28)

Suggested Lifestyles for the Firstborn

1. You can have high standards and expectations without being a perfectionist. Try loosening up a bit and don't expect that others should adhere to the same standards that you set for yourself.
2. When people try to influence you to take risks, stick to your first inclination, which is probably to be cautious.
3. Take pride in your ability to be responsible.
4. Learn to laugh at yourself. Sometimes you'll be wrong—just admit it! We were born to lead.

CHAPTER 6

Prayers for Victorious Living

Christ urged us to pray; without prayer and fasting, certain problems that affect us will not cease to exist. We have been given a name to call upon, and that name is JESUS CHRIST! No matter the situation you are going through, Jesus is ever present to put an end to all demonic attacks, sickness, and poverty; His name and His blood is sufficient to set you free and get your life back on track.

We have some prayer points for Christians and those in need of deliverance. These prayer points listed here are to help put you on the path to a strong prayer life. They are not some special kind of prayers that you have to pray mandatorily; everything written is in conformity with the Bible and the things of God.

We have all been taught how to pray by Jesus Christ Himself; He says we should ask anything in His name and we shall receive. Once again, these prayers are listed here to help set you on a course to a powerful prayer life; it is not a ritualistic type of prayer—you can pray as you are led or as you wish to. Remember, where the Spirit of the Lord is, there is liberty.

Note: To pray the prayer of deliverance, you have to be strong, and it is also advisable to have people pray with you in order to avoid unwanted attacks. This message goes out especially to those who have demonic oppression or possession. If you need further prayers, you can see the pastor of your church or contact us using the contact information given in this manual.

Prayer Points for Victorious Living

1. *Thank God.* Learn to give thanks and praises to God always, at all times, and in every situation.
2. *Confess you sins.* Confess your sins to God and ask for forgiveness and cleansing in the blood of Jesus Christ. We have all sinned, so ask God to forgive your sins in words, actions, and/or thoughts, which is actually the most dangerous of all.

Prayer Points for Change

1. Every evil handwriting written by the devil, demons, or anyone against me concerning my life, destiny, career, family, children, etc.—I erase such handwriting in the name of Jesus.
2. Dear God, just as You made a way for the children of Israel, make a way for me where there seems to be no way in the name of Jesus.
3. Dear God, every enemy of progress fighting against my success or progress in life—physically or spiritually in any form or realm—I command the earth to open its mouth and swallow them up in the name of Jesus.
4. Every evil spoken word against me in open or in secret, I condemn by the precious blood of Jesus in the name of Jesus.
5. Dear God, every wickedness sent or targeted against me in the physical or spiritual realm, I command such wickedness to perish by the fire of the Holy Ghost in the name of Jesus.
6. Every demonic oppression affecting my life, I break its power and hold over my life in the name of Jesus.
7. Every spirit of oppression and depression destroying my life, making life unbearable for me, I bind and cast you out of my life into the bottomless pit in the name of Jesus.

8. Every covenant made knowingly or unknowingly by me, my parents, or within my generation that is evil and does not bring glory to God, I break such covenants in the name of Jesus.

9. I shall succeed, I shall progress in the name of Jesus.

10. I seal my life, marriage, career, etc., with the blood of Jesus in the name of Jesus.

11. Dear God, preserve my soul from evil and destruction in the name of Jesus.

12. I cover myself with the blood of Jesus against any plan of evil or destruction or death in the name of Jesus. (Make this your daily prayer for protection.)

13. Dear God, I know You have a plan for my life. Father, let me walk in the plan You've made for me and my spouse, children, etc., in the name of Jesus.

14. Dear God, let Your plan for my life come to manifestation in the name of Jesus.

15. Dear God, increase Your love in me in the name of Jesus.

16. Dear God, make me RAW (ready, able, and willing) to show and practice Your love and Your will according to Your commandment in the name of Jesus.

17. Dear God, speak to me today—I want to know the right plan and direction I should follow in the name of Jesus.

18. Dear God, set me on fire for You in the name of Jesus.

19. Dear God, grant me Your divine favor to succeed and stand out amongst the crowd in the name of Jesus.

20. Pray and begin to decree good things into your life, whatever you want Him to do for you in area of your life.

> Thou shalt also decree a thing, and it shall
> be established unto thee: and the light shall shine
> upon thy ways. (Job 22:28)

Prayer Points for Claiming My God-Given Destiny

1. I erase and nullify every incantation, ritual, and witchcraft powers against my destiny in Jesus's name.
2. I render null and void the influence of destiny swallowers in Jesus's name.
3. I nullify all household wickedness, struggling to rearrange my destiny, in Jesus's name.
4. My destiny is attached to God; therefore, I decree that I can never fail in Jesus's name.
5. I bring under captivity every power waging war against my destiny in Jesus's name.
6. I overthrow every satanic rearrangement programmed against my destiny in Jesus's name.
7. I refuse to accept satanic substitute for my destiny in Jesus's name.
8. I reject and terminate every power drawing powers from the heavenlies against my destiny in Jesus's name.
9. Today, I raise up an altar of continuous prosperity upon my destiny in Jesus's name.
10. I reject every satanic rearrangement of my destiny in Jesus's name.
11. I reject and renounce destiny-demoting names and I nullify their evil effects upon my destiny in Jesus's name.
12. The designs of my enemy against my destiny shall be destroyed in Jesus's name.
13. Every conspiracy of darkness against my destiny, scatter by fire in Jesus's name.
14. You evil strongman attached to my destiny, be bound in Jesus's name.

Prayer Points for Uprooting Inherited and Foundational Problems

As a firstborn, it helps to constantly pray the following prayer points:

1. Lord, I absolve myself of every evil ancestral curse and inheritance in the name of Jesus.
2. You evil ancestral pattern of failure in the life of the firstborn, I disconnect myself from you in the name of Jesus.
3. I release myself from all collective family captivity in the name of Jesus.
4. I command all evil family altars crying against my life to be consumed by the fire of the Holy Spirit in the name of Jesus.
5. Inherited family curses hanging over my destiny, be nullified in the name of Jesus.
6. I terminate inherited wars and unrest in my life in the name of Jesus.
7. I command all foundational problems in my life to be rooted out in the name of Jesus.
8. I root out barrenness and poverty in my life in the name of Jesus.
9. God, exempt me from all inherited iniquities of my family's lineage by fire in the name of Jesus.
10. Every evil flow of destiny pollutants from my family into my life, I command to dry up from its source in the name of Jesus.

Prayer Points for Breaking Hidden and General Curses

Christ hath redeemed us from the curse of
the law, being made a curse for us: for it is written, Cursed is every one that hangeth on a tree:
That the blessing of Abraham might come on

the Gentiles through Christ Jesus; that we might
receive the promise of the Spirit through faith.
(Galatians 3:13–14)

A curse is a violent expression of evil (intent) upon others. It is a word, phrase, or sentence calling for punishment, injury, or destruction of something or on somebody. It is uttering a wish of evil against someone.

A curse is an evil pronouncement propelling one's life in a direction not originally intended. Curses are words put together to torment a person with great calamity.

A curse is an invisible barrier that keeps people away from the plan of God for their lives. Curses are oral pronouncements that bring about harm.

Curses could be self-inflicted, based on disobedience to the Word (and Spirit) of God, inherited, transferred, and pronounced on an individual by wicked people.

When hidden curses are in place, you find yourself taking wrong steps and decisions, and the spirit of failure will be in full operation.

1. I break and cancel every curse placed upon me by my parents either due to their carelessness, in anger, or by mistake in the name of Jesus!
2. By the resurrection power, I deactivate the power of all curses affecting my ancestral family as a result of their sin and disobedience to God in the name of Jesus!
3. I break and cancel every curse, evil pronouncement, spells, hexes, enchantment, bewitchment, and incantations placed upon me by the kingdom of darkness in the name of Jesus!
4. I break and revoke every blood and soul-tie covenants and yokes attached to those curses in the name of Jesus!
5. I purge myself of all evil foods I have eaten with the blood of Jesus and I purify myself with the fire of the Holy Ghost in the name of Jesus!

6. Father, please forgive me and may the blood of Jesus cleanse me from every disobedience that introduced curses into my life in the name of Jesus!

7. Holy Ghost, revoke every caterpillar and cankerworms that are destroying my finances as a result of the curses in the book of Malachi in the name of Jesus!

8. Lord, let the blood of Jesus speak for me regarding any of the curses recorded in the Bible that is affecting my progress in the name of Jesus!

9. Holy Spirit, deliver me from all self-inflicted curses that were pronounced either consciously or unconsciously in the name of Jesus!

10. I retrieve and cancel every word I have spoken at any time of my life that has brought judgment upon me in the name of Jesus!

11. All power implementing evil curses over my life, you are defeated in the name of Jesus!

12. I return to sender every curse pronounced over my life by demonic agents of darkness in the name of Jesus!

13. I plead the blood of Jesus over all evil pronouncements affecting my destiny in the name of Jesus!

14. By the power in the blood of Jesus, I break all self-imposed curses working against my progress in the name of Jesus!

15. God of Elijah, arise and deliver me from every curse of polygamy in my foundation in the name of Jesus!

16. By the blood of Jesus, I break every curse used by the strongmen of my father's house in the name of Jesus!

17. By the blood of Jesus, I break every curse used by the strongmen of my mother's house in the name of Jesus!

18. By the power in the blood of Jesus, I break every curse of untimely death working in my family line in the name of Jesus!

19. By the power in the blood of Jesus, I break every curse of wrong marriages in my family line and I decree that I am not your candidate in the name of Jesus!

20. By the power in the blood of Jesus, I terminate every curse of stubborn limitations in my family line in the name of Jesus!

21. Under the covenant of the blood of Jesus, I stand to neutralize and deactivate the power of every curse inflicted on me at any point in time because Christ has redeemed me from the curse of the law.

Prayer For Breaking Generational Curses

A generational curse is a curse that has been activated into one's life from birth, aligning that person to the same calamities affecting his or her generation. It is a curse you don't work for; it automatically takes over the life of a person.

> Thou shalt not make unto thee any graven image, or any likeness of anything that is in heaven above, or that is in the earth beneath, or that is in the water under the earth. Thou shalt not bow down thyself to them, nor serve them: for I the Lord thy God am a jealous God, visiting the iniquity of the fathers upon the children unto the third and fourth generation of them that hate me; And shewing mercy unto thousands of them that love me, and keep my commandments. (Exodus 20:4–6)

1. Holy Ghost, scatter all powers inherited from my parents, propelling my life toward a direction not commissioned by God, in the name of Jesus!

2. I destroy all evil powers implementing evil decrees into my life in the name of Jesus!

3. I command all powers of darkness assigned to implement failure in my life to come out (of my life) in the name of Jesus!

4. I scatter every gathering of the ungodly against me (physically or spiritually) from my conception till this present day in the name of Jesus!

5. Every form of evil information brought against me from the kingdom of darkness, I cancel you in the name of Jesus!

6. I abort every operation of the forces of darkness commissioned against me to monitor my progress in life in the name of Jesus!

7. (Lay your right hand on your head and your other hand on your stomach.) Every evil operation, evil nature, and evil habits inherited from my lineage, lose your hold in the name of Jesus!

8. Every initiation, dedication, and manipulation that has yoked me into all forms of generational bondage, be broken now and forever in the name of Jesus!

9. Let every incantation, evil decrees, and curses uttered against me from my birth become impotent in the name of Jesus!

10. All curses affecting the members of my family, lose your grip and hold over my life in the name of Jesus!

11. I paralyze the activities of every strongman ruling over my generation and working against my progress in the name of Jesus!

12. Let every generational curse that is affecting my destiny be broken in the name of Jesus!

13. I renounce all curses originating from my ancestors and I denounce the power of those curses in the name of Jesus!

14. I break all evil pronouncements propelling my life to the same type of failure, misfortune, poverty, and material lack suffered by my ancestors in the name of Jesus!

15. Holy Ghost, disconnect me from all curses placed upon my ancestral family that is now affecting my progress in the name of Jesus!

16. By the power in the blood of Jesus, I paralyze all foundational curses working against my divine destiny in the name of Jesus!

17. By the power in the blood of Jesus, I break all generational curses of poverty mutilating against my breakthroughs in the name of Jesus!

18. By the power in the blood of the Lamb, I paralyze every parental curse hindering my progress in the name of Jesus!

19. By the power in the blood of the Lamb, I break the generational curse of idolatry working against my life in the name of Jesus!

20. I release myself and my family from all collective captivity of idolatry in the place of my birth in the wonderful name of Jesus!

21. By the power in the blood of Jesus, I release myself and my family from every collective captivity of innocent blood that was shed by my parents up to ten generations ago in the name of Jesus!

22. I break the power of every foundational curse placed on the place of my birth in the name of Jesus!

23. By the power in the blood of Jesus, I paralyze every curse of "aborted destinies" in my family line and I declare that "I am not your CANDIDATE" in the name of Jesus!

Prayer Points—Lord, Fight For Me!

1. Lord, forgive us for our sins and the sins of our fathers in the name of Jesus!

2. Lord, help us to return to You and keep Your commandments in the name of Jesus!

3. Lord, let Your favor and mercy be upon us in the name of Jesus!

4. My God will commission me this year for His divine purpose in the name of Jesus!

5. Hear me, O my God! Let the hands of my enemies be weakened in the work that they are carrying out against me; it will not be done in the name of Jesus!

6. Lord, expose my enemies and bring their plot against me to nothing in the name of Jesus!

7. Lord, strengthen my hands to perform the work you have assigned to me in the name of Jesus!

8. Remember me, O God, for good in the name of Jesus!

9. The Lord will build a wall around me in the name of Jesus!

10. O Lord, deal with my enemies for me while I am doing the work You committed into my hands in the name of Jesus!

11. My enemies will be shocked and amazed to see how God will surprise me in the name of Jesus!

12. Lord, redeem me by Your great power and by Your strong hand according to Your promise in the name of Jesus!

13. Lord, give me favor in the sight of my helpers in the name of Jesus!

14. God of heaven, cause me to prosper in the name of Jesus!

15. Lord, remember Your servants and spare them in Your mercy in the name of Jesus!

16. Hear me, O my God, for I am despised and turn my enemy's reproach onto their own heads in the name of Jesus!

17. Lord, send my enemies into the land of captivity in the name of Jesus!

18. I bless Your name, O Lord, for Your goodness upon my life and I thank You for answered prayers in the name of Jesus!

SCRIPTURAL DECLARATION OF VICTORY THROUGH THE BLOOD OF JESUS

1. Through the blood of Jesus, I am redeemed out of the hand of the devil **(Ephesians 1:7)**.

2. Through the blood of Jesus, all my sins are forgiven **(Psalm 107:2)**.

3. The blood of Jesus, God's Son, continually cleanses me from all sin **(1 John 1:7)**.

4. Through the blood of Jesus, I am justified, made righteous, *just as if I'd* never sinned **(Romans 5:9)**.

5. Through the blood of Jesus, I am sanctified, made holy, and set apart unto God **(Hebrews 13:12)**.

6. My body is the temple of the Holy Spirit, redeemed and cleansed by the blood of Jesus **(1 Corinthians 6:19–20)**.
7. Satan has no place in or power over me through the blood of Jesus and the Word of God **(Revelation 12:11)**.
8. In Him (Jesus) we have redemption (deliverance and salvation) through His blood, the remission (forgiveness) of our offenses (shortcomings and trespasses), in accordance with the riches and the generosity of His gracious favor, which He lavished upon us with every kind of wisdom and understanding (practical insight and prudence) **(Ephesians 1:7–8)**.
9. Let the redeemed of the Lord say so, whom He has delivered from the hand of the adversary **(Psalm 107:2)**.
10. But if we are (really) walking and living in the Light as He (Himself) is the Light, we have (true) unbroken fellowship with one another, and the blood of Jesus Christ, His Son, cleanses (removes) us from all guilt and sin (keeps us clean from sin in all of its forms and manifestations) **(1 John 1:7)**.
11. Therefore, since we are now justified (acquitted, made righteous, and brought into a right relationship with God) by Christ's blood, how much more (certain) shall we be saved by Him from the indignation and wrath of God **(Romans 5:9)**?
12. Therefore, Jesus also suffered and died outside the (city's) gate in order that He might purify and consecrate (sanctify) the people through (the shedding of) His own blood and set them apart as holy (unto God) **(Hebrews 13:12)**.
13. Do you not know that your body is the temple (the very sanctuary) of the Holy Spirit Who lives with you, Whom you have received (as a gift) from God? You are not your own **(1 Corinthians 6:19)**.
14. You were bought with a price (purchased with preciousness and paid for, made His own). So then, honor (your) God and bring glory to Him in your body **(1 Corinthians 6:20)**.

15. And they have overcome (conquered) him by means of the blood of the Lamb and by the utterance of their testimony, for they did not love or cling to life even when faced with death (holding their lives cheap till they had to die for their witnessing) **(Revelation 12:11)**.

16. In the name of Jesus, O Lord, baptize me with the fire of deliverance in the name of Jesus!

17. All demonic spirits attached to all covenants and curses, I bind you and command you to come out of my life in the name of Jesus!

18. Father, let the blood of Jesus Christ erase all my sins that opened the doors to the curses recorded in the Bible in the name of Jesus!

19. By the power of resurrection, I reverse every negative decree already signed against me and that can affect me in any form in the name of Jesus!

20. Father, reverse every negative order placed over my destiny in the name of Jesus!

21. Holy Spirit, let Your voice respond on my behalf wherever my name is written or mentioned in the name of Jesus!

22. Holy Spirit, confuse my enemies in their own camp in the name of Jesus!

23. Let the power of God tear down everything the devil has put together concerning my name in the name of Jesus!

24. Under the new covenant—that is, the covenant of the Blood of Jesus—I renounce all the evil works I have done in the lives of innocent people through my membership with these demonic associations, and I ask the Almighty God to forgive me and cleanse me with the blood of Jesus in the name of Jesus!

25. I request the blood of Jesus to flush out my system, purify my body, and cleanse me from all evil things I have eaten in any of the demonic cults or associations in the name of Jesus!

26. Wherever my name has been initiated either consciously or unconsciously, I withdraw and cancel my name from their registers with the blood of Jesus in the name of Jesus!

27. By the power in the blood of Jesus, I withdraw any part of my body or blood deposited on their evil altars in the name of Jesus!

28. I withdraw pictures, objects, presentations, food, sacrifices, money, children, wife, husband, clothes, images, and any other personal belongings from the altars of the forces of darkness in the name of Jesus!

29. I return any weapon (physical or spiritual) belonging to the kingdom of darkness that I was a part of, and I also return any other properties for the execution of satanic duties at my disposal in the name of Jesus!

30. Holy Spirit, build a wall of fire around me and let there be a permanent disconnection between the satanic kingdom and me in the name of Jesus!

31. By the blood of Jesus, I cancel and erase every evil mark, incision, tattoo, and writing inserted on my body as a result of my participation with the forces of darkness in the name of Jesus!

32. I break all covenants that I have undertaken for my children, grandchildren, and generations after me in the name of Jesus!

33. By the power in the blood of Jesus, I renounce and denounce every dedication of my destiny to any river, mountain, or idol in the place of my birth in the name of Jesus!

34. By the power in the blood of Jesus, I renounce and denounce every initiation into occultism by my parents and/or grandparents in the name of Jesus!

35. By the power in the Blood of Jesus, I cancel every dedication or covenant with family idols, evil trees, forests, markets, road junctions, and so on in the name of Jesus!

36. Anyone monitoring me through a satanic glass or device, I command that glass or device to be broken in the name of Jesus!

God bless you!
I believe the power of God will work in your life to
set you free as you diligently study this teaching and
faithfully pray using the prayer points listed above.
Victory is yours in Jesus's name.

—Rev. James A. Solomon

Rev. James A. Solomon is the President of Jesus People's Revival Ministries Inc., as well as the General Overseer and Senior Pastor of Jesus Family Chapel, with 38+ branches, in Nigeria, the United Kingdom and several other countries. The international headquarters for both ministries is based in Atlanta, Georgia, in the United States of America, where he currently resides.

Rev. Solomon is a man who is truly gifted with an extraordinary anointing on the subject of Spiritual Warfare, Healing and Deliverance. In his efforts to serve the body of Christ beyond his own ministries, he also serves as director for the West African Regional Directorate of the International Accelerated Missions (I.A.M.), a network of missionary churches based in New York.

Rev. Solomon started from very humble beginnings in his native country of Nigeria, West Africa, way back in the 1980s. With his team of ministers and due to popular demand, he has taken the revelation of Spiritual Warfare and Deliverance to massive venues such as the stadium domes in the major cities of Nigeria. He has also conducted a series of conferences, and organized quarterly Deliverance Night Services in the United Kingdom, Europe, Canada, Japan and all over the United States. Many have received freedom from satanic bondage and oppression at these quarterly deliverance services. He is in high demand as a guest minister in many crusades and conferences.